FROM
STARDUST

MADE FROM STARDUST

Exploring the place of human beings within creation

Denis Edwards

CollinsDove
A Division of HarperCollins*Publishers*

Published by Collins Dove
A Division of HarperCollins*Publishers* (Australia) Pty Ltd
22-24 Joseph Street
North Blackburn, Victoria 3130

First published 1992

Designed by William Hung
Cover design by William Hung
Cover 'The Garden of the Stars' Charles Blackman
Typeset by Collins Dove Desktop Typesetting
Printed in Australia by Griffin Press

The National Library of Australia
Cataloguing-in-Publication Data:
Edwards, Denis, 1943–

Made from stardust.

Bibliography.
ISBN 1 86371 037 X.

1. Theology. 1 Title.

230

Cover: *The Garden of the Stars*. Charles Blackman
The Garden of the Stars. Diptych, each panel 122x153cm. Oil on canvas.
This painting was exhibited in Tokyo Central Museum, Japan during
Autumn 1989. It is now in a private collection.
Charles Blackman is a leading Australian artist. He held his first one-man
exhibition in Melbourne in 1953. Associated with the Antipodean group of
painters (1959); won the Rubinstein Travelling Scholarship (1960) and the
Dyason Endowment (1960). His work is represented in all major galleries
and in many private collections.
Charles Blackman kindly donated the fee for the use of the reproduction of
his painting, *The Garden of the Stars*, to the Parish of the Sacred Heart,
West St Kilda, Melbourne, to help the homeless.

Acknowledgements
Our thanks go to those who have given us permission to reproduce
copyright material in this book. Particular sources of print material are
acknowledged in the text.
Every effort has been made to contact the copyright holders of text material.
The editor and publisher apologise in those cases where this has proved
impossible.

The ecological crisis and the advances made by late twentieth century science offer serious challenges to the human community as we face the third millennium. How do we understand ourselves as part of an expanding cosmos and the evolutionary history of life on earth? How do we as human beings understand ourselves in relationship to the Big Bang and nucleosynthesis in stars? Denis Edwards in *Made from Stardust* attempts to answer these questions. By listening to what the scriptures have to say about creation, and reflecting on the findings of contemporary science in the light of these biblical insights, Denis Edwards develops a view of human beings in relationship to other creatures. This view seeks to be faithful to both the Christian tradition and science, and to hold together a commitment to both social justice and ecology.

What results is a book that provides a theological grounding for Christian involvement in the ecological movement.

Denis Edwards is a priest of the Archdiocese of Adelaide. He works as the Theological consultant to the Archbishop, and as a lecturer in systematic theology in the Adelaide College of Divinity. He is the author of *Jesus and the Cosmos, Called to be Church in Australia, What Are They Saying About Salvation? Human Experience of God.*

ACKNOWLEDGEMENTS

Quotations from the Bible are from the *New Revised Standard Version* Oxford University Press, New York, 1989, copyright held by the Division of Christian Education of the National Council of Churches of Christ in the United States of America. Quotations from the following works are by permission of the publishers: Bill Neidjie's *Story About Feeling* Magabala Books, Broome, 1989; *The Collected Works of St. John of the Cross*, tr. by Kieran Kavanaugh and Otilio Rodriguez, ICS, Washington, D.C., 1979; *St. Francis of Assisi: Writings and Early Biographies*, Marion A Habig (ed.), Franciscan Herald Press, Chicago, 1983.

I owe special thanks to Alistair Blake, who generously made time to discuss with me a number of issues addressed in this book, from the perspective of his own field of physics. I am very grateful to those who have been friends and companions in this work.

CONTENTS

*

CHAPTER 1

A new time calls for a new theological approach

At the end of the twentieth century, we are moving into a new phase of evolutionary history. We confront a crisis never before faced in the three-and-a-half billion years of life on Earth. We have come to understand that human beings have the power to destroy or to save life on our planet.

The hole in the ozone layer, global warming, the destruction of the Earth's great forests, the loss of topsoil, the spread of deserts, the pollution of our atmosphere, land, rivers and seas - all of this is like a great cry of distress from the Earth itself, warning us that we have arrived at an unparalleled moment of choice in the history of our planet.

This moment is characterised by enormous population growth, and an unjust international economic structure which maintains the gap between the poor majority, who do not have even the necessities of life, and the rich few, who consume far too much of the Earth's resources.[1] But this time is also characterised by new possibilities of global solidarity. It is a time of new vision and new resources. A central dimension of this is the beginning of an historic shift in consciousness with regard to equity and justice for women. We have begun to understand the long history of the repression of women and the impoverishment of life which is related to it. We can see the links between this history and the current ecological crisis. The increasing presence of women in leadership positions in public life, combined with a renewed appreciation of relational values and mutuality, offers new hope that we may be able to develop our commitment to global community.

The choice for life in the crisis we face with regard to the life-systems of our planet will demand a conversion to a new ecologically based approach to existence on Earth. Humanity is being challenged to opt consciously for a way of life which respects the interconnectedness of all creatures. In this context, the human community faces an urgent task in self-understanding: how are we to see ourselves in relationship to other creatures on this planet and beyond it?

Part of the answer to this questions comes, I believe, in listening to and learning from Aboriginal voices, like that of Bill Neidjie. In apprenticeship to Aboriginal culture, we can glean insight from a spiritual heritage which integrates the whole of life, so that stars and trees and people are seen as closely interconnected:

> Tree, grass, star...
> because star and tree working with you.
> We got blood pressure
> but same thing...spirit on your body,
> but e working with you.
> Even nice wind e blow...having a sleep...
> because that spirit e with you.
>
> Listen carefully this, you can hear me.
> I'm telling you because earth just like mother
> and father or brother of you.
> That tree same thing.

Your body, my body I suppose,
I'm same as you...anyone.
Tree working when you sleeping and dream.

This story e can listen carefully, e can listen slow.
If you in city well I suppose lot of houses,
you can't hardly look this star
but might be one night you look.
Have a look star because that's the feeling.
String, blood...through your body.

That star e working there...see?
E working. I can see.
Some of them small, you can't hardly see.
Always at night, if you lie down...
look careful, e working... see?
when you sleep...blood e pumping.

So you look...e go pink, e come white.
See im work? E work.
In the night you dream, lay down,
that star e working for you.
Tree...grass...

I love it tree because e love me too.
E watching me same as you
tree e working with your body, my body,
e working with us.
While you sleep e working.
Daylight when you walking around, e work too.[2]

Later in this book I will return to the relationship between stars and trees and life-blood, and it will become evident how much congruence there is between the traditional wisdom and insight of Bill Neidjie and the discoveries of contemporary science.

In some circles, the environmental crisis we face is blamed on traditional religion, particularly Judaism and Christianity, and the saying in the first creation story of the Book of Genesis: 'Be fruitful and multiply, and fill the earth and subdue it; and have dominion over the fish of the sea and over the birds of the air and over every living thing that moves upon the earth' (Gen.1:28).

There is no doubt that this text has been taken out of its context and misused to legitimate the exploitation of nature. In the next section of this book, I will attempt an interpretation of Genesis 1:28 which does respect its context. At this stage, however, it is important to note that the use of this text to license global pollution and the squandering of resources does not represent the original meaning of the text in the priestly tradition of ancient Israel, nor the way the text was understood in the early Church and in the Middle Ages.[3] It is a post-colonial, post-industrial, ideological usage that stems mainly from the rise of capitalism in the West.

Some Christians have contributed to this misuse of Genesis 1:28, and the churches have, by and large, failed to protest against it vigorously – at least until recent times.

I will argue that the present situation of our planet calls the whole Christian community to a radical conversion of mind and heart, to a renewed theology of creation, and to a positive commitment to the integrity of all creation.

At a deeper level, Christianity is accused of an unthinking and dangerous focus on human beings as the centre of everything (anthropocentrism). It is argued that Christianity's emphasis on the dignity of the human person, and its insistence that human beings are made in the image of God, have led to a narrow focus on human beings as the centre of creation, accompanied by an exploitative attitude towards other creatures. It is argued, as well, that Christianity's orientation towards the future, and its emphasis on the new heaven and new earth at the end of history, have been transformed, in secular culture, into a dangerous myth of endless economic progress.

It must be admitted that a distorted Christian theology has been used to support an exploitative approach to creation. It is also true, however, that within the Christian tradition, in the Bible itself, as well as in the writings of the great theologians and mystics, there is another, much more holistic, approach to creation. Here we find a joy in, and celebration of, the variety of creatures as representing the bounty and diversity of the Creator.[4] In this wide stream of Christian tradition, there is an understanding of the close relationship between all creatures, and a sense of the community of all creatures in God. Christianity at its best is surely not centred on humanity (anthropocentrism), nor simply on all living creatures (biocentrism), but on all things in God. I believe that what we need today are new theological efforts which will respond, in the light of this tradition, to the ecological crisis and our new scientific understandings, offering alternatives to narrow anthropocentric approaches.

If a narrow anthropocentrism is one dangerous extreme then the other is surely the view that humankind is no more than one species among many. Some of our contemporaries, rightly alarmed at the damage humankind has done to the Earth, go so far as to describe human beings as a scourge upon the Earth, as a plague out of control, or as a demonic presence on the planet.[5] I will argue that a Christian theology cannot accept such positions. If human beings have no more value or dignity than an insect or a worm then the quest for global justice is seriously undermined. Such a view of the human person is not congruent with the Christian theology of creation and incarnation.

9

It is obvious that if contemporary theology finds both anthropocentric and reductionist views of the human person inadequate and dangerous, then it has the responsibility to contribute to the search for a more adequate understanding of the place of human beings within creation. What is required is a theology of human beings within creation which is faithful to both the Christian tradition and twentieth-century science, and which is capable of holding together a serious commitment to both ecology and justice for the poor of the Earth.

In an attempt to build such a theology, it will be helpful to listen to what the Scriptures have to say about creation, and then, in the light of these biblical insights and the wider Christian tradition, to listen to and reflect upon the findings of contemporary science.[6]

FURTHER REFLECTIONS

1. How would you describe the present moment of our global history? What do you see as the fundamental challenges we face at the end of second millennium? What do you see as key resources? What provides the basis for hope?

2. To what extent do you think Christianity is anthropocentric? How do you see Christianity's contribution to Western civilisation, and our present ecological crisis?

3. What elements of your faith undergird your own commitment to social justice? What inspires your commitment to an ecological view of the world? How do you understand the relationship between justice and ecology?

CHAPTER 2

The Biblical vision of creation

The theme of creation is one of the foundations of biblical faith. Far from being confined to the first eleven chapters of Genesis, it is a major theme of many of the biblical writings.

In biblical faith, the God who liberates the chosen people from slavery in Egypt is the same God who creates all things. Creation and salvation find their unity in the God who acts in both. This finds clear expression in the Psalms, where the one God is praised as creator and redeemer. In the Christian Scriptures, God's liberating activity in Jesus is seen as a new creation, and the meaning and purpose of God's creation is seen as salvation and the reconciliation of all things in Christ.

A biblical theology of creation, then, would need to embrace the whole Bible, including not only Genesis, but many other books, above all the second part of Isaiah, the Psalms, Job, Proverbs, Sirach, Wisdom, Paul's letters, Colossians, Ephesians, Hebrews, first Peter, John's Gospel and Revelation. I will focus on the story of creation in Genesis 1:1–2:4a and its theological meaning for us today, and follow this with very brief discussions of Genesis 2:4b–11, Psalm 104, and some of the New Testament text concerning creation.

THE STORY OF CREATION IN GENESIS 1:1–2:4

In many Christian churches, the familiar story of the creation of the whole universe in seven days is read with great solemnity at each Easter Vigil. For the assembled community this is a powerful affirmation that the whole of God's creation is caught up in the transforming power of the resurrection.

Most biblical scholars believe that this creation story had its origin in priestly circles between the seventh and sixth centuries BC. By the time it was being written, there were already many other stories of origin available, including the ancient Hebrew stories told in Genesis 2–3, as well as the creation stories of neighbouring peoples, such as the Enuma Elish and the Gilgamesh myths from Babylon.

The priestly author shaped this new account of creation in a very specific way to bring out particular theological insights. The fundamental structure is that of a week of work, with God resting on the seventh day. Eight works of creation take place in the first six days, and so we find God accomplishing a double task on days three and six:

Day 1   Light, and day and night
Day 2   The dome of the sky to hold back the waters above
Day 3   Separation of the earth from the seas
        Vegetation brought forth from the earth
Day 4   The great lights in the dome of the sky
Day 5   Sea creatures and birds
Day 6   The land animals
        Humankind, made in the image of God
Day 7   God rests, and blesses and makes holy the seventh day.

The story makes it very clear that creation occurs through the command of God. In each work of creation we find this same rhythmic sequence:

1 an introduction to the command: 'God said …'
2 the command: 'Let there be …'
3 the accomplishment: 'And it was so'
4 the judgement : 'God saw that it was good'
5 the time sequence: 'And there was evening and there was morning, the…day.'[7]

At the end of each day's work, God declares creation good and, at the end of the sixth day we are told, 'God saw everything that he had made, and indeed, it was very good' (1:31). Three times God blesses what has been created, the sea creatures and the birds (1:22), humankind (1:28) and the seventh day (2:3). The continuous refrain of the goodness of creation and the solemn blessings challenge our exploitative culture, and they also challenge some Christian views of the material universe.

The story of the creation of the world is divided into the creation of the world as a living space (1:1-10), the creation of plants and animals (1:11-25), and the creation of humankind (1:26-31). Human beings are presented as the climax of creation: 'in the image of God he created them; male and female he created them.' The description of humankind as the image of God is repeated and emphasised. God blesses humankind, tells them to 'fill the earth and subdue it', and to 'have dominion over' the animals. The language used here is harsh. It is language of the rule of kings.

What does all this mean for us today? What are we to learn from it? What is the theological message, the salvific truth expressed in this story? Simply because it is a powerful and beautiful story, it can communicate at many levels beyond the range of conceptual thinking, but this does not absolve us from the task of attempting to discern the difference between time-conditioned assumptions and the enduring theological truths being taught in the Genesis story.[8]

What is obviously time-conditioned is the world-view assumed by the author. The assumptions about cosmology, what might be called the scientific understanding, of the sixth century BC are not in any way binding on believers today. The cosmology that the writer takes for granted – the idea that there is a great mass of water above us, which is separated from us by the great dome of the sky to which are attached the Sun and Moon and the stars – is not part of the theological truth of the Bible. Believers today are not bound to the cosmology of the ancient writers.

Nor are they committed in any way to the order, or to the time-frame, of the seven days of creation. The structure of the seven days is a literary construct which serves a theological purpose. Those who shaped the Book of Genesis did not intend to teach any one sequence of things in the beginning. This is made perfectly clear when we find that Genesis includes alongside Genesis 1:1-2:4 another story of origins in Genesis 2-3, with a quite different order of events.

If modern believers are not bound to the scientific assumptions of the sixth century BC, nor to the order of events and the time-scale of Genesis 1, what do they hold to as the enduring teaching of this story? In the next section I will attempt to bring together a summary of some of the key teachings of the opening chapter of the Bible. In the rest of this book these insights, along with others from the biblical and theological tradition, will be the light by which I will read the story of the universe as told by contemporary science.

SOME KEY THEOLOGICAL INSIGHTS FROM THE FIRST CREATION STORY

The first creation story of the Bible (Gen.1:1–2:4a) has an important theological message for today's world. Some of the key aspects of this message can be summarised in the following eight points:

1. **The story is a powerful proclamation that the fundamental relationship between the one God and the whole world is to be understood as an ongoing relationship between a Creator and creatures.** Realities that contemporaries of the author worshipped as divine (the Sun, the Moon, the stars and the fertility of nature) are assessed here as simply creatures. Bruce Vawter comments on this: 'We are so far removed from the world of Genesis that we can scarcely comprehend how revolutionary was such a statement uttered to those who were habituated to a universe whose heavens were peopled with gods and demons, benign and malign tutelary spirits.[9] The story of creation in Genesis 1 teaches that all things have an enduring creaturely relationship with a Creator who while being engaged at the very heart of creation yet transcends it. Creation is not seen as a casual event or an accident, but as the work of a Creator with a powerful purpose in creating. Walter Brueggemann suggest that the fundamental relationship that this story teaches can be summarised in the sentence: 'The Creator creates creation.'[10]

2 **The relationship between God and creatures is not to be understood in mechanistic terms.** God is not thought of as a clockmaker, constructing a machine which will run on automatically. Rather, creation is understood in terms of a relationship. God creates by

word, freely and graciously, setting up a relationship of commitment and trust.

3 **The text proclaims that creation is a source of delight to the Creator**. Delight is part of the structure of reality, for both Creator and creatures (See Ps.65:8; Ps.104:26; Prov.8:30–31).[11] At the completion of each work of creation we find the phrase: 'God saw that it was good,' and when all is finished we are told: 'God saw everything that he had made, and indeed, it was very good.' The Hebrew word *tob*, which we translate 'good' also means 'beautiful'. It can also mean 'ordered' and 'purposeful'. God finds all of creation beautiful. In the wider Jewish tradition, human beings and other creatures, too, delight in what God creates and respond with praise. (Ps. 104, 148).

4 God blesses living creatures (1:22), humankind (1:28), and the Sabbath (2:3). Claus Westermann has shown that this blessing refers to the generative power of life and well-being that God has freely placed within creation.12 Fertility and all that it means in terms of mating, conceiving, bringing to birth, and nurturing is blessed and empowered by God. This blessing binds humankind and other living creatures together in one organic world of physical life which is presented as thoroughly positive. The blessing points to the interconnectedness of all living things and to the dynamism for life at the heart of our world which has its source in God.

5. **Human beings are made in the image of God**. What does this mean? Over the centuries, commentators have suggested various attributes of human beings which make us like God. Some contemporary

commentators focus on the 'dominion' human beings have over animals, and the idea that human beings are representatives of God.[13] I believe that Westermann has made a convincing case that a fundamental meaning of the phrase 'image of God' is that God has created creatures able to be in interpersonal relationship with God's self. The Creator creates a community of creatures that corresponds to God's self, beings to whom God can speak, and who can hear God speaking. In fact, God twice speaks to humanity in this account (1:28 and 1:29-30). Humankind is created 'so that something can happen' between God and the human community.[14] Karl Barth has described the special character of the human person as being 'a Thou which can be addressed by God and an I which is responsible before God'.[15]

6 **Human beings are given dominion over other animals and told to subdue the Earth.** This is the harsh language of kingly rule.[16] It must be admitted that it is dangerous language in the context of the late twentieth century. In its original context, however, it would have had a liberating intention - to stress the dignity of the human person. In creation narratives of the surrounding world, human beings were created to be slaves, to bear the yoke of the gods. Furthermore, nature itself was understood as threatening and full of malevolent spirits. This command reflects an experience of the natural world as threatening and at times alien, and a conviction that the human vocation is the 'kingly' one of bringing human intelligence, courage and work to bear on the land so that herds might flourish, crops grow, and cities be built. In a Jewish world, this kingly role was understood in

relationship to God's shepherding rule, and the model of the shepherd-king, David. And, as Pope John Paul II has consistently pointed out, the language of dominion must always be interpreted in the light of the understanding that humankind is made in the image of God the Creator, who takes delight in all creatures.17 There is no right here to play God, no justification for ruthless exploitation and irresponsible destruction of animal or plant life. Such behaviour is totally immoral and a sin against creation and the Creator. Today this text can be understood as a time-conditioned expression which, nevertheless, contains a profound and enduring truth: human beings are created to cultivate the Earth and to take part in the unfolding of God's creation intelligently and responsibly.

7 **Human beings are created male and female.** Sexuality is understood as good and sexual difference is part of creation. Humankind is a community of male and female, and this communal life, and sexual life, expresses the divine image. Both male and female are bearers of the divine image. While God transcends male and female, and God's generativity transcends human mothering and fathering, both are limited, but appropriate, images for the Creator.[18]

8 **On the seventh day God rests.** Work and rest are part of the Creator's plan. The artificial structure of the seven days shows that the days of work have their goal in a different day, that the everyday leads to the special day. There is here an obvious reference to the institution of the Sabbath in Israel. But there is a wider reference to the rhythm of creation and recreation, work and rest, the everyday and the day of celebration. The celebration of a day of rest was an

act of trust 'in this God who is confident enough to rest'. It is 'an assertion that life does not depend upon our feverish activity of self-securing, but that there can be a pause in which life is given to us simply as gift'.[19] There is also a deeper understanding that the whole story of creation will reach its goal in that rest in God which the rest of the seventh day suggests.[20]

These eight points are simply one attempt to summarise some of the principle theological teachings that emerge from a study of the first creation story in the Bible. As has been said already, this is a far from complete picture of what the Bible has to say about creation.

FURTHER BIBLICAL INSIGHTS ON CREATION

The biblical picture of creation would be incomplete without the account of sin and God's ongoing fidelity, contained in the stories of origin which begin in Genesis 2:4b and conclude in Genesis 11.[21] Here we find an ancient story which tells of the forming of the first man out of clay, the garden of Eden, the creation of animals and birds from the ground, the creation of woman from a rib of the man, the union between man and woman, the eating of forbidden fruits, the consequences of sin and the expulsion from the garden (2-3). This is followed by the tragedy of Cain and Abel (4), the story of the flood and the covenant with Noah (6-9), and the story of the tower of Babel (11).

These stories are rich and complex, but for the purposes of this work, the theology contained in them can be summarised under four points: God creates human beings and acts with love towards them; human beings sin and find themselves alienated from God, from their own selves, from one another, and from the Earth itself; sin results in punishment; God shows compassion and offers a further blessing and promise.[22]

In this context, we find further important reflections on the relationship between human beings and other creatures. The command given to the newly made human being in Genesis 2:15 is 'to cultivate and care for' the garden. Obviously, the relationship in Eden between humankind and other creatures is one of joy in creation and responsible care. In these stories, too, we hear of God's commitment to living creatures and to the Earth itself. After the great flood, God makes a covenant not only with Noah, but will all living creatures, and we are told that the rainbow is the sign of the everlasting covenant established between God and the Earth:

> God said 'This is the sign of the covenant that I make between me and you and every living creature that is with you, for all future generations: I have set my bow in the clouds, and it shall be a sign of the covenant between me and the earth. When I bring clouds over the earth and the bow is seen in the clouds, I will remember my covenant that is between me and you and every living creature of all flesh. When the bow is in the clouds, I will see it and remember the everlasting covenant between God and every living creature of all flesh that is on the earth.' God said to Noah, 'This is that sign of the covenant that I have established between me and all flesh that is on the earth' (Gen.9:12–17).

The relationship between God and all creatures is also the theme of Psalm 104. Here we find another way of approaching creation, a magnificent hymn of praise celebrating God's wisdom and power revealed in the diversity of creation. God is manifest in the cosmos:

wrapped in light as with a garment
you stretch out the heavens like a tent
you set the beams of your chambers on the waters,
you make the clouds your chariot,
you ride on the wings of the wind,
you make the winds your messengers,
fire and flame your ministers (Ps. 104:2-4).

The great forces of the Earth are understood as the expressions of God's presence and God's activity. God is engaged with creation, sustaining and empowering all things, from the springs of water to the wild goats, from the storks nesting in the fir trees to the setting sun:

You make springs gush forth in the valleys;
they flow between the hills,
giving drink to every wild animal;
the wild asses quench their thirst.
By the streams the birds of the air have their habitation;
they sing among the branches.
From your lofty abode you water the mountains;
the earth is satisfied with the fruit of your work.

You cause the grass to grow for the cattle,
and plants for people to use,
to bring forth food from the earth
and wine to gladden the human heart,
oil to make the face shine,
and bread to strengthen the human heart.
The trees of the Lord are watered abundantly,
the cedars of Lebanon that he planted.
In them the birds build their nests;
the stork has its home in the fir trees.
The high mountains are for the wild goats;
the rocks are a refuge for the coneys.
You have made the moon to mark the seasons;
the sun knows its time for setting.
You make darkness, and it is night,

when all the animals of the forest come creeping out
(Ps. 104:10-20).

God is being celebrated as at the heart of creation, revealed in its beauty, enabling its fertility and abundance. Everything is held in existence by God: 'when you take away their breath they die...when you send forth your spirit they are created' (Ps.104:29-30). This psalm celebrates the whole of creation in all its interconnectedness and diversity, and it finds God's creative activity manifest in all things and empowering all things. The response of the psalmist can only be: 'I will sing to the lord as long as I live; I will sing praise to my God while I have being' (Ps. 104:33).

For Christian believers, God's creative activity continues in and through the life, death and resurrection of Jesus. Creation and salvation in Jesus of Nazareth are not separate or competing mysteries, but rather two distinct aspects of God's one engagement with the world – 'In the beginning was the Word, and the Word was with God, and the Word was God...all things came into being through him...and the Word became flesh and lived among us' (Jn.1:1-14).

In the Pauline writing, Christ is understood as a new Adam (Rom. 5:17-21), and we are understood as a 'new creation' in Christ (II Cor. 5:17; Gal.6:15). Salvation in Christ is seen against the background of the creation stories in the opening chapters of Genesis, and the repeated statement that human beings are made in the image and likeness of God.[23] Although Paul's explicit focus is on the justification of human beings in Christ, he sees the future of the created world as intimately bound up with the future of humanity, and so he describes how 'creation waits with eager longing for the revealing of the children of God' (Rom.8:19). Paul tells us that 'the whole of creation has been groaning in labour pains until now; and not only the creation, but we ourselves, who have the first fruits of the Spirit, groan inwardly while we wait for adoption, the redemption of our bodies' (Rom.8:22-23).

In Colossians we find that 'all things' are created 'in Jesus'.

> He is the image of the invisible God, the firstborn of all creation; for in him all things in heaven and on earth were created, things visible and invisible, whether thrones or dominions or rulers or powers - all things have been created through him and for him. He himself is before all things and in him all things hold together (1:15-17).

In Jesus Christ 'all the fullness of God was pleased to dwell, and through him God was pleased to reconcile to himself all things, whether on earth or in heaven, by making peace through the blood of the cross' (1:19-20). The whole cosmos - 'all things, whether on earth or in heaven' - is to find reconciliation and right relationship in the risen Christ. The saving action of God in Jesus of Nazareth is the unfolding of God's purpose in creation, and it is also the beginning of the transformation of all creation.

Ephesians describes the meaning of God's purpose in creation in these words: 'With all wisdom and insight he has made known to us the mystery of his will, according to his good pleasure that he set forth in Christ, as a plan for the fullness of time, to gather up all things in him, things in heaven and things on earth' (Eph.1:9-10). Creation does have a meaning and a purpose. The purpose is the unification of all creatures, the whole known cosmos, in Christ. This is the 'mystery' of God's will, the salvation, unification and gathering up of all creation in Christ.

In the last book of the Bible we have a marvellous vision of 'a new heaven and a new earth', and of a 'new Jerusalem', a place where God will dwell among God's people, wiping away every tear from their eyes. In this vision, the one seated on the throne says: 'See, I am making all things new...I am the Alpha and the Omega, the beginning and the end' (Rev. 21:1-6). This vision points to a future for us and for the universe in which all things are transformed and renewed.

The early Christian community, above all in the hymns scattered through the New Testament (e.g. Jn.1:1-18; Col.1:15-20; Heb. 1:3-4), celebrated the risen Christ at the heart of cosmic processes. The first believers were convinced that God created all things 'in' and 'through' the Word. They saw God's purposeful action as including both creation and incarnation. Furthermore, they were convinced that the death and resurrection of Jesus were concerned not with the salvation of human beings in isolation from the rest of creation, but with cosmic reconciliation.

This incomplete sketch of the biblical teaching on creation provides a basis for a theological exploration of the place of human beings within the integrity of creation. It does not answer scientific questions about how creation occurs. A late twentieth-century theology will need to listen to, and learn from, late twentieth-century science, but it will do this with theological insight derived from the biblical and doctrinal tradition. This is the task for the next section of this book.

FURTHER REFLECTION

1. How do you understand the biblical view of creation? What is the heart of it for you? What approach to creation has come through your own experience of Church?

2. What do you think about the theology of blessing? How might it be explored? Do you see any ways in which the concept of the sabbath might take on new meaning for an ecological age?

3. What do you think about the theory of evolution? Do you think that the Bible gives any direction on this issue? Are there any problems in bringing the theory of evolution and biblical faith together? Are there advantages?

4. How do you see the relationship between salvation in Jesus Christ and the material universe? Does salvation include other creatures as well as humans?

CHAPTER 3

**Towards a theological
view of human beings in
inter-relationship with
all other creatures**

Both the need for an ecological approach to life and the emergence of a new cosmology make it necessary to attempt to build a new theological picture of the human person in relationship to the rest of creation.

To do this means taking seriously scientific models such as the 'big bang' theory, and reflecting on them in the light of Christian faith. These models are based upon observation, and also partly upon internal consistency and elegance. My interest is in the broad lines of theories such as the 'big bang'. I am well aware that, although such a model represents the best understanding we have at present, it is incomplete and will certainly by modified in the light of new discoveries. It is my conviction, however, that this must not deter the theologian from theological reflection upon current understandings. Both contemporary cosmology and a contemporary theology will necessarily be somewhat provisional in their findings, but in my judgement this is entirely appropriate. Certainly, theology is something which must always be done anew - as it attempts, in a new context, to grasp the mystery and meaning of our lives and of the universe in the light of Christian faith.

I will attempt to build a theological picture of humankind within creation by considering human beings under six aspects: as springing from the primordial fireball, as made from stardust, as an integral part of the evolutionary history of life on Earth, as companions to all other creatures in an Earth community, as the cosmos come to self-awareness, and as creation invited into relationship with the Creator.

1
HUMAN BEINGS – SPRINGING FROM THE PRIMORDIAL FIREBALL

There is widespread agreement among astronomers and cosmologists that the universe as we know it had its origin about fifteen billion years ago, when space and time expanded rapidly from an extremely compressed, hot and dense state, in an explosion of enormous energy known as the 'big bang'.[24]

Scientists use a combination of astronomical observation, experiments with high-energy particle accelerators, and theoretical physics, to trace the history of the universe back to within the first fraction of a second of the 'big bang'. Theories concerning what happened in the first fraction of a second are highly speculative, although they are built upon experimental work and the theoretical work of quantum physics.

Most cosmologists are convinced that there is reasonably strong evidence for the general picture of the 'big bang' itself. Stephen Hawking, for example, writes: 'we can be fairly confident that we have the right picture, at least back to about one second after the big bang'.[25] Recent work by astronomers on the positions of galaxies has revealed unexpected structures, and a great degree of 'clumpiness', in our universe, and this has called into question a number of assumptions about how galaxies were formed. By and large, however, the great majority of cosmologists still hold to the overall structure of the 'big bang' theory as the most plausible explanation of how the universe began.[26]

Within the first second of the 'big bang', an enormous amount of cosmic history occurred. This was because the temperature was massive, more than 10^{32} degrees Kelvin, and because it plummeted down to about a million degrees within the first minute. As the temperature fell past certain key values, conditions changed quickly from one state to another. The story of the unfolding universe is a story of 'eras', each of which is determined by the progressively falling temperature.[27]

In the unimaginable temperature and density of the first second, the universe existed as a tiny, rapidly expanding 'soup' of energy-matter. Many theorists hold that in this period the universe went through a stage of rapid inflation in which it expanded in size more than a trillion trillion times.[28] At the end of this **Inflation Era** there was a release of enormous energy in the form of radiation – the beginning of the great fireball.

The fireball was dominated by radiation in the form of high energy photons. In the extraordinary high temperature within the first second, photons and particles interacted in equilibrium. Energetic photons could decay into particles and antiparticles of matter, which would then annihilate one another, and form new photon pairs.

The concept of 'antimatter' and of 'antiparticles' needs some explanation. Matter can be created in a laboratory, but it is always accompanied by an equivalent amount of antimatter. For example, the creation of a particle like an electron is always accompanied by a symmetrical antiparticle (a positron) which has the same mass as the electron, but an opposite electrical charge. This raises the problem of why the universe seems to consist of almost 100 per cent matter. Where is all the equivalent antimatter? Cosmologists answer that in the 'big bang', the symmetry between matter and antimatter was broken, and a slight excess of matter was produced.

As the temperature dropped in the early universe, radiation became less energetic. By the end of the first second, the photons did not have sufficient energy to maintain the supply of particles and antiparticles, which were continually annihilating one another. This lack of production, plus the annihilation process, would have meant the end of all of matter, except that there was already a tiny lack of symmetry between particles and antiparticles frozen into the universe from the Inflation Era. There were slightly more particles than antiparticles. It is calculated that there were a billion and one particles of matter for each billion particles of antimatter.[29] By the end of the first second, most of the antimatter of the universe had been annihilated with matter, leaving only this slight excess of matter. Later, this 'left-over' matter would come into its own. The whole material universe, including humankind, comes from it.

The period between one minute and five minutes after the 'big bang' is called the **Nucleosynthesis Era**. The temperature had dropped to the level at which nuclear reactions could occur. Conditions were right for the creation of the first atomic nuclei, although it was still far too hot for atoms to form. Protons and neutrons fused to form the nuclei of varieties of hydrogen and helium. By and large, heavier elements were not formed because the temperature continued to drop too quickly to allow for further fusion. When scientists model what they think happened in the 'big bang', they estimate that about 25 per cent of the emerging plasma would have been made up of helium nuclei, and about 75 per cent would have been destined to become the nuclei of hydrogen atoms. Such estimates reflect the level of these elements in the observed universe today.

After the first five minutes, the universe entered a new phase of its history, the Radiation Era, which was to last for about half a million years. In this period, the universe continued to expand and cool, but no major transitions occurred. The universe was still dominated by radiation, and matter was opaque to radiation and remained coupled to it. The cosmos existed in the form of a glowing plasma of ionised hydrogen and helium. It was still too hot for atoms to form.

At the end of this half million-year period the temperature had dropped to something like the temperature of the sun's surface and electrons could unite with protons to form hydrogen atoms. Matter and energy were uncoupled, and matter began to emerge as the dominant component of the expanding universe. The radiation era of the 'big bang' was over. It was followed by the **Era of Matter**.

In this next great stage in the unfolding of the universe, space became transparent, clouds of hydrogen and helium took shape, and the long process of the formation of the galaxies began. This period of the predominance of matter, the stellar period, has already lasted for more than ten billion years. It has been an era of comparatively leisurely unfolding as the universe has continued to expand and cool. In this period the original ball of fire has been transformed into an expanding world of atoms, molecules, galaxies and stars, living organisms and conscious human beings.

In 1965, Arno Penzias and Robert Wilson, researchers at the Bell Telephone Laboratories in New Jersey, accidentally made the discovery that the universe is filled with microwave radiation.[30] This microwave radiation has a temperature of 2.7 degrees above absolute zero.[31] It seems clear that this radiation is the afterglow of the radiation era of the 'big bang'. It is a remnant from the primordial fireball of the universe.

We ourselves are remnants from the fireball. Without the emergence of hydrogen nuclei in the first minutes of the fireball, and the formation of hydrogen atoms at the end of this period, the stars would not burn, there would be no water anywhere, and no life would be possible. The human community springs from the fireball which carried within itself the potentiality for the universe which includes us and is unfolding around us.

The primordial fireball, blazing forth with unimaginable energy, contained within itself all that would ever emerge into being. As Thomas Berry writes, the fireball was 'the present in its primordial form', just as the present is 'the fireball in its explicated form'.[32] Conscious human beings have sprung from the original fireball. They are the elaboration of the potential already contained in the great primordial blaze of energy.

God's creative action is not something extrinsic to this process. Rather, God has chosen to create in such a way that all possibilities are already contained within the original fireball. And the Creator is at work in the whole process whereby the universe unfolds from its fiery beginning, empowering it from within.

2
HUMAN BEINGS –
MADE FROM STARDUST

Our bodies are made up of atoms of carbon, hydrogen,

oxygen and other elements, strung together in a complex whole, shaped by the genetic information encoded in DNA molecules.

But what of the atoms that make up our bodies? Where do they come from? According to astrophysicists, these atoms had their origin long ago in complex processes that occur in stars. This creative process is called nucleosynthesis. Stars can be thought of as great nuclear fusion reactors in which hydrogen nuclei are the fundamental fuel, and heavier elements are the outcome.

This theory was outlined in 1957 by four scientists, Margaret Burbidge, Geoffrey Burbidge, William Fowler and Fred Hoyle, in a famous paper 'Synthesis of the Elements in Stars.'[33] According to this theory, the first generation of stars was formed from great clouds of hydrogen, as they coalesced under the influence of gravity. In the intense heat which built up in the depths of these protostars, hydrogen was converted to helium. Successive fusion processes in stars enabled the light elements, hydrogen and helium, to be converted into heavier ones, like carbon, and then into more complex nuclei like nitrogen, oxygen and neon. As the stars aged and their cores heated, heavier elements could be synthesised up to iron. Iron's nuclear structure does not allow it to fuse into heavier elements. Some of the heavy elements produced in these stars flowed out into space This material has been recycled in second- and third-generation stars like our Sun.

Over the last thirty years this theory has been widely accepted by scientists and, in 1983, William Fowler received the Nobel prize for his part in developing it. In 1987, the theory received further confirmation when scientists were able to observe a supernova at first hand. They detected gamma rays and neutrinos coming from supernova SN1987A, and these discoveries confirmed predictions made in the theory of nucleosynthesis.

In a star like the Sun, hydrogen is converted to deuterium in a nuclear fusion process, with a release of energy which keeps the Sun extremely hot. In a further fusion process, deuterium is converted to helium. The release of nuclear energy generates enough outward pressure to keep the Sun more or less stable against the force of gravity. In the process, the Sun radiates enormous energy in the form of heat and light.

According to Bernard Lovell, in the Sun 'some 564 million tons of hydrogen are transformed into 560 million tons of helium' during each second. This process represents the conversion of 'only a tenth of 1 per cent of its mass every ten million years'.[34] The Sun has been at work for about 5 billion years, and it is estimated that it is about half way through its active life.

Hydrogen and much of the helium in the universe were produced in the 'big bang'. They are fossils from the fiery origins of the universe, but no significant quantities of elements heavier than helium came from this source. All the other elements are cooked in the stars.[35] Over the lifetime of an older star, hydrogen and helium will be transformed into a storehouse of heavy chemical elements.

These heavy elements are like spent nuclear ash. As a star ages, its nuclear reactions begin to falter. It may lose its capacity to support itself against its own gravity, and collapse in upon itself. Then a burst of energy from the core may blast the outer layers of the spent star into space in a supernova explosion. Heavy elements are catapulted out into the galaxy, and the galaxy is enriched with the trace elements needed for the formation of planets like the Earth and the bodies of living creatures.

Our bodies are made from these elements. As Paul Davies says we are 'built from the fossilized debris of once-bright stars that annihilated themselves aeons before the Earth or Sun existed'.[36]

All the chemical elements in the human hand and the human brain were forged in the furnaces of stars. The four most abundant elements in our bodies are oxygen (65 per cent), carbon (18 per cent), hydrogen (10 per cent), and nitrogen (3.3 per cent). There are smaller amounts of other elements like calcium, phosphorus, potassium, sulphur, sodium, chlorine, magnesium, iron and manganese. All the atoms that make up our bodies, except for the primordial hydrogen, have been produced in the stars. David Ellyard has described this process in these words:

> In this way was made all the iron we now find in our blood, all the phosphorus and calcium that strengthens our bones, all the sodium and potassium that drive signals along our nerves. Atoms so formed are thrown off into space by aged stars in their death throes. Natural forces recycle them into new stars, into planets and plants and people. We are all made of stardust.[37]

The heavy elements of the Sun are recycled material from older stars. The material of which the Earth is made and the atoms that make up human beings have come from an earlier generation of stars which have exploded as supernovae and scattered heavy elements across space. The debris of dying stars has enriched the mixture of gases from which new stars, planets, and people are born. We are the grandchildren of supernovae. We are indeed made from stardust.[38]

3
HUMAN BEINGS – AN INTEGRAL PART OF THE EVOLUTIONARY HISTORY OF LIFE ON EARTH

The human community on Earth is interconnected with everything else in the universe through the primordial fireball, and through our common origin in the depths of the stars. God has created us in such a way that we are radically connected to all other matter and to all the forces at work in the universe. But humankind is also part of the great network of living organisms on this planet.

Every living creature on Earth depends upon, and is shaped by, the DNA molecule, which had its origin between three and four billion years ago. Our human genetic structure bears the imprint of the conditions our ancestors met over many ages. Our bodies can be thought of as living fossils, relics of the evolutionary movement that began with the first expression of life in blue-green algae, and continues in us.

We still have no way of accounting for the transition from inert matter to the first living organism, and the emergence of the amazing DNA molecule. We do not know enough about what happened between the formation of the Earth (about 4.6 billion years ago) and the appearance of life, the earliest form of which appears to be blue-green algae. The remains of cells of blue-green algae have been discovered at Warrawoona in Australia in rocks which are 3.5 billion years old.[39]

Oxygen in the Earth's atmosphere seems to have arrived on the scene about the same time. There was an intimate relationship between the emerging life-forms and the atmosphere. Photosynthesis meant that the amount of oxygen could be maintained at about 21 per cent, and further life-systems could emerge.

Two billion years ago, life existed in the form of sponges, algae and fungi. Less than a billion years ago, the first animal life seems to have appeared in the form of marine invertebrates. The higher forms of plant life emerged about 400 million years ago. By the end of the Palaeozoic period (230 million years ago), the ocean was populated by bony fish, rays and sharks, and there is evidence of the first vertebrates on land in the form of fish-like amphibians. Reptiles dominated the Earth during the Mezozoic period (230–65 million years ago), and mammals and birds made their appearance as well (about 150 million years ago).

The first primates appeared at the beginning of the Canozoic period (about 65 million years ago). There is evidence of *Homo Erectus*, with a large cranium and the capacity to use fire and tools, from about 2 million years ago. Modern humankind (*Homo sapiens sapiens*) seems to have emerged in various places at roughly the same time (between 30,000 and 40,000 years ago). Evidence points to what is probably modern humankind in Australia about 47,000 years ago.

There is a family connection between the first forms of life and modern human beings. All living beings are interconnected through evolutionary relationships. Darwin's theory, transformed in the light of twentieth-century genetics, forms the basis for the development of the new biology of the late twentieth century.

Although not all biologists accept the adequacy of the neo-Darwinian description of the mechanism of evolution (natural selection and random mutation), there is widespread agreement about evolution itself. As

Arthur Peacocke states: 'The proposition of evolution – that all forms of life, current and extinct, are interconnected through evolutionary relationships – is not in dispute among biologists.'[40]

In fact, Peacocke points out, late twentieth-century science has confirmed the theory of evolution in various ways. Biochemistry has demonstrated that there are fundamental similarities at the molecular level between all living creatures from bacteria to human beings. Furthermore, molecular biology has demonstrated 'not only that the prime carriers of hereditary information in all living organisms are the nucleic acids (DNA and RNA) but also that the code that translated the information from base sequences in proteins (and thence to their structure and function) was the *same* in *all* living organisms.'[41] Since this code is arbitrary in the same way that a language is arbitrary, Peacocke concludes that its universality can be explained only as a result of evolution. It points to a family relationship between all living creatures.

These living creatures are interconnected with the atmosphere, the water systems, and the soil in such a way that each part of the system depends upon the other. Together they form a biosphere which makes life possible and which has the possibility of sustaining life. Recently, James Lovelock has offered the hypothesis that the whole planet should be seen as one self-sustaining system of life, which he calls 'Gaia'.[42] Whether one uses the concept of 'Gaia' or not, there is no denying the delicate inter-relationships between all the life-systems on our planet and the land, the oceans, the rivers and the atmosphere.

Recent studies have tended to suggest that emergence of life is not to be explained simply by random molecular shuffling. The work of Ilya Prigogine, Manfred Eigen, and other researchers, has pointed to a widespread tendency within nature towards self-organisation.[43] It is becoming clearer that matter and energy in far-from-equilibrium open systems have a tendency to seek out higher and higher levels of organisation and complexity. It is possible that there are as yet unknown organising principles in nature which will explain the appearance of life, as well as the increasing complexity of living creatures.[44]

Human creatures, with developed intellects and a capacity for self-awareness, emerge as part of this self-organising movement of the cosmos.[45] They share a common heritage with the whole cosmos, in their origin in the primeval fireball, in being made from stardust, and in their evolutionary relationship with all living creatures on Earth.

4
HUMAN BEINGS – COMPANIONS TO OTHER CREATURES IN AN EARTH COMMUNITY

Charles Birch, in his recent book *On Purpose*, challenges the mechanistic worldview, in which the world is seen as a great machine, made up of components or building blocks, all of which obey mechanical laws which can be predicted and measured. He offers, as an alternative, what he calls a postmodern ecological worldview, based upon the idea of relationships.

This ecological worldview affirms a real continuity between human beings and the rest of the living world. It values individual entities, from protons to people, not simply for their usefulness to human beings (their 'instrumental value') but for their 'intrinsic' value. In this view, things have value in themselves. Birch connects the intrinsic value of creatures to the possession of a degree of self-determination and feeling. He finds these characteristics present in some way not only in animals, but also in other beings:

> The proposition of the ecological model is that no line is to be drawn anywhere down the line of what we call living organisms, and thence down through molecules, atoms and electrons and protons. This is not to argue for consciousness as such all the way down the line, but for some form of awareness or attenuated feeling associated with some degree of freedom to choose. Human experience is seen as a high-level exemplification of reality in general, that is of individual entities from protons to people.[46]

It seems to me that there are difficulties with Birch's attempt to link the idea of the intrinsic value of things with the concept of feeling. Even if something does not 'feel' it can still have instrinsic value. In theological terms, intrinsic value needs to be grounded in God's creative presence and action in the diversity of creatures. I am convinced, nevertheless, that the worldview proposed by Charles Birch is extremely important for our global future.

Fundamentally, he tells us, everything is inter-related. Molecules and cells respond to their environment, and, in some sense, must be seen as subjects. They should be understood as in continuity with the human mind with its much more developed responses and subjectivity. He suggests we need to move from seeing the world, at its most basic level, as made up of substances which obey mechanical laws to seeing it as a network of events and relationships. Birch insists that not all creatures are equal in ethical value – the scale of consciousness gives priority to human beings over an insect or a virus. Nevertheless, humankind is understood as radically interconnected with all other creatures.

Quantum mechanics tells us that what we call elementary particles are really sets of relationships. Relationships constitute the very essence of things. Electrons and atoms and human beings are what they are because of a network of relationships.

In quantum mechanics we learn that the human observer cannot predict with accuracy how a particle will react. Its response is in some sense a 'free' one. Probability is a permanent feature of the quantum world. Subatomic particles do not exist with certainty at definite places and times. Rather they show a well-defined 'tendency' to occur. Furthermore, we know from Heisenberg's uncertainty principle that when we seek to observe or measure a particle like an electron, we may measure the electron's position or its momentum, but we cannot do both at the same time.

The act of observing or measuring has an impact upon the particle. In preparation for an observation, a particle is isolated, in some sense called into being. If the preparation is modified the properties of the particle will change. The observer cannot stand outside the quantum world, but is drawn in as a participant. This opens up great unanswered questions about the relationship between the world of sub-atomic particles and the mind.[47]

Quantum physicists insist that the most fundamental thing about the world of matter is the inter-relationship between things. The great founding figure of the Copenhagen school of quantum mechanics, Niels Bohr, has said that 'isolated material particles are abstractions, their properties being definable and observable only through their interaction with other systems.'[48]

David Bohm, an opponent of the Copenhagen school, agrees. He says that particles should not be seen as the fundamental reality, as independent building blocks. It is rather the interconnectedness of the whole universe that is the fundamental reality, and the relatively independently behaving parts are particular, contingent forms within this whole. We are invited to view the world as 'a universal flux of events and processes'.[49]

Fritjof Capra writes that 'quantum theory forces us to see the universe not as a collection of physical objects, but rather as a complicated web of relations between the various parts and the whole'.[50]

The discoveries of quantum physics offer some important ideas for a new understanding of humankind within creation: they deny that the world is made up of fundamentally separate objects; they demonstrate that inter-relationship is fundamental to a description of the universe; they include human consciousness as part of the description of the world.

A theological view of the human person within creation can only be a theology of inter-relatedness. We are bodily, connected creatures, profoundly inter-related with the rest of creation in our origin, in our present existence and in God's future for us. Like all other creatures our origin is in the fireball of the 'big bang' and in the furnaces at the centre of stars. God's creative action does not cease with the 'big bang', but sustains and empowers the whole expanding cosmos, and evolutionary history on Earth, in all its interconnectedness. The saving, liberating action of God in Jesus of Nazareth is a promise of a future in which God will embrace not just the human community, but in a mysterious way all of creation, in a 'new heaven and a new Earth.'

It is an urgent task for Christian thinkers to find ways to express the truth of our relatedness to other creatures, and to help us to see how we human beings are part of an ecological whole on the Earth. What is needed according to Sallie McFague is a new 'aesthetic sensibility' towards the cosmos, which 'values what is unselfishly, with a sense of delight in others for their own sakes. This appreciation and delight is a necessary step in turning from an anthropocentric to an ecological sensibility.[51] She argues that 'to feel in the depths of our being that we are part and parcel of the evolutionary ecosystem of our cosmos is a prerequisite for contemporary Christian theology'.[52]

Thomas Berry is someone who has led the way in this work. One of his suggestions is that we need to ponder how we are interconnected with the rest of the universe through our genetic coding. This coding appears as a spontaneous force arising from within us, providing authentic guidance for wise human conduct. Of course we need to respond to this inner direction with critical reason, yet also with the knowledge that, ultimately, our genetic coding comes from that mysterious source which empowers the whole unfolding universe.

Our genetic coding provides guidance in the organic functions of our body, in the transforming of food into energy, in the functioning of our senses, and in our imaginative, emotional and intellectual life. It enables the body to heal itself. These spontaneities from within enable us to speak and to create, and provide the context for our relationship with the divine.[53]

Humankind has ignored its relationship with the Earth and ignored its genetic coding. The result has been an industrial human culture which has become exploitative and dangerous. Berry sees our fundamental task at the end of the twentieth century as the proper relating of human culture (our 'cultural coding') to the imperatives of our genetic coding. We have to learn again to listen to our bodies, and to the Earth, and to see ourselves as companions with other creatures on a fragile planet.

This theme of companionship is fundamental as we Christians attempt to envision ourselves in an inter-related universe. Theologians who have been struggling with these ideas have suggested that what is needed for an ecological theology is the development of the two related ideas of 'sacramentality', and 'companionship'.[54]

The idea that all creatures are 'companions' to women and men is not a new one. It has long been recognised by Francis of Assisi and the other great mystics of our tradition. Over a long period of time, Matthew Fox has been drawing attention to the 'creation spirituality' of the great medieval spiritual writers like Hildegard of Bingen, Meister Eckhart and Julian of Norwich as part of the project of developing contemporary creation spirituality.[55] I will draw attention here to two of the great mystics, Francis of Assissi and John of the Cross. Francis could see Sun, Moon and stars, wind, water and fire, mother Earth who sustains and governs us, and even death itself, as brothers and sisters, companions and common creatures before God:

> All praise be yours, my Lord, through all that you have made,
> And first my lord Brother Sun,
> Who brings the day; and light you give to us through him.
> How beautiful is he, how radiant in all his splendour!
> Of you, Most High, he bears the likeness.

All praise be yours, my Lord, through Sister Moon and
Stars;
In the heavens you have made them, bright
And precious and fair.
All praise be yours, my Lord, through Brothers Wind and
Air,
And fair and stormy, all the weather's moods,
By which you cherish all that you have made.
All praise be yours, my Lord, through Sister Water,
So useful, lowly, precious and pure.
All praise be yours, my Lord, through Brother Fire,
Through whom you brighten up the night.
How beautiful is he, how gay! Full of power and strength.
All praise be yours, my Lord through Sister Earth, our
mother,
Who feeds us in her sovereignty and produces
various fruits with coloured flowers and herbs.[56]

As Sean McDonagh has said, the memory of Francis in
our world today is a 'healing, reconciling and creative
one' and he is a happy choice as the patron saint of
ecologists.[57]

John of the Cross finds all of creation in the Beloved,
and the Beloved in all of creation:

My Beloved is the mountains
And lonely wooded valleys,
Strange islands,
And resounding rivers,
The whistling of love-stirring breezes,

The tranquil night
At the time of the rising dawn,
Silent music,
Sounding solitude,
The supper that refreshes and deepens love.

In part of his commentary on these verses, John of the Cross States:

> In this same way the soul perceives in that tranquil wisdom that all creatures, higher and lower ones alike, according to what each in itself has received from God, raise their voice in testimony to what God is. She beholds that each in its own way, bearing God within itself according to its capacity, magnifies God. And thus all these voices from one voice of music praising the grandeur, wisdom, and wonderful knowledge of God.[58]

All of creation, and every creature, is 'sacramental' in the sense that it embodies and expresses something of God. The diversity of creatures symbolises the abundance of God, who is present to each creature as the creature power which enables it to be and to become. I would see this as a fundamental basis for understanding the 'intrinsic value' of creatures.

5
HUMAN BEINGS – THE UNIVERSE COME TO SELF-AWARENESS

Human beings are the product of the 'big bang', they are made of elements forged in the stars, and they are the result of three-and-a-half billion years of evolutionary history here on Earth. They are profoundly interconnected with other creatures. But they are more than this. What is distinctive about women and men is that they are creation come to self-consciousness at a particular time and place.

This does not rule out, of course, the possibility that there are other creatures elsewhere in our universe who are also matter come to self-consciousness. But, granted this possibility, we can and must still say that matter has come to consciousness in humankind. Matter comes to itself in conscious thought, self-reflection, communication, culture, science, art, community and love. Women and men are beings in whom the great diversity of the universe can rejoice in itself in self-awareness.

There is a remarkable consensus among a number of theologians and scientists about this way of seeing the human person. Many years ago, Teilhard de Chardin, borrowing a phrase from Julian Huxley, described human beings as discovering that they were nothing other than 'evolution become conscious of itself'.[59] Thomas Berry speaks of the human as 'that being in whom the grand diversity of the universe celebrates itself in conscious self-awareness'.[60] Sallie McFague writes that our human status and responsibility are not limited to our personal bodies, nor to the human world, but extend to all bodily reality since 'We are that part of the cosmos where the cosmos itself comes to consciousness'.[61]

Carl Sagan sees human beings as 'the local embodiment of a Cosmos grown to self-awareness'.[62] Paul Davies describes the sequence of events from the fireball to atoms, stars, planets and life, and concludes: 'Thus, the universe became self-aware'.[63] Arthur Peacocke writes that in human beings 'matter has become aware of itself, of its past, and of its unfulfilled potentialities'.[64] He also says that 'in human beings part of the world has become conscious of itself and consciously and actively responds to its surroundings'.[65]

Karl Rahner, too, suggests that the human person can be understood as the cosmos come to consciousness of itself.[66] Rahner argues that it is of the very nature of the material universe to develop towards consciousness. Human beings are part of the cosmos, part of the one story of evolution. The material universe finds itself in them. If human beings are the universe come to self-awareness, then this gives a new perspective, and new depth to the relationship that human beings have with all of matter, with every giant galaxy millions of light years away, and with every subatomic particle. Human beings are all of this come to self-awareness at a particular place and time.

We remain profoundly linked to every other creature. We are part of the supernova far out in space. We share its heritage and its history. We are intimately linked to the whole life-system of our planet, and the complex inter-relationship between living creatures and the atmosphere, the soil and the water systems. We are part of all this and, in a real sense, we are all of this come to consciousness in a particular locality.

Human community, and the communication between the peoples of the Earth, are part of the one story of the cosmos. The unfolding of the universe continues now in human community and in human history.[67] It is manifest in growing global solidarity, in science and culture, and in human interaction with the rest of creation. Human beings are the ones in whom the whole cosmos presses forward towards self-consciousness. In this we have an authentic basis for a proper understanding of human dignity within creation.[68]

Thomas Berry in a summary paragraph expresses beautifully much of what I have been saying here about human beings in the midst of creation:

> The story of the universe is the story of the emergence of a galactic system in which each new level of expression emerges through the urgency of self-transcendence. Hydrogen in the presence of some millions of degrees of heat emerges into helium. After the stars take shape as

oceans of fire in the heavens, they go through a sequence of transformations. Some eventually explode into the stardust out of which the solar system and the earth take shape. Earth gives unique expression of itself in its rock and crystalline structures and in the variety and splendour of living forms, until humans appear at the moment in which the unfolding universe becomes conscious of itself. The human emerges not only as an earthling but as a worldling. We bear the universe in our being as the universe bears us in its being. The two have a total presence to each other and to that deeper mystery out of which both the universe and ourselves have emerged.[69]

I have discussed at some length the inter-relationship between ourselves and the rest of the universe, and our relationship with God has been part of this discussion, but it is time now to turn more explicitly to a consideration of our presence to 'that deeper mystery' out of which human beings and the whole universe have been born.

6
HUMAN BEINGS – CREATION BECOME ABLE TO RESPOND TO GOD'S SELF-OFFERING

At the end of a recent book concerned with self-organising principles at work in the universe, Paul Davies writes:

> The very fact that the universe *is* creative, and that the laws have permitted complex structures to emerge and develop to the point of consciousness – in other words, that the universe has organized its own self-awareness – is for me powerful evidence that there is 'something going on' behind it all. The impression of design is

> overwhelming. Science may explain all the processes
> whereby the universe evolves its own destiny, but that
> still leaves room for there to be a meaning behind
> existence.[70]

Theologians are happy to leave science to explain 'all the processes whereby the universe evolves its own destiny'.

Theology's task is to attempt to articulate what Davies calls the 'something going on' behind it all. What is going on here, Christians believe, is that the whole process is empowered from within by a God who is the dynamic reality at the heart of the whole process of the self-organising universe.[71]

Christian theology reflects, in the light of its tradition, upon the story of the unfolding universe told by contemporary science, including the 'big bang', the formation of galaxies, nucleosynthesis in stars, the formation of the Earth, the emergence of life in the form of blue-green algae, photosynthesis, the advent of animal life in the oceans and then on land, the period of the great reptiles and the first mammals, the emergence of the primates and the evolution of human beings. It sees all of this as sustained and empowered from within by a mysterious being who turns towards us with a boundless personal love.

The unfolding of the universe, its capacity to leap forward across thresholds, its size and beauty, the marvellous abundance of life on our planet, the emergence of self-conscious beings capable of love and community – all of these are understood as manifestations of the divine presence which empowers the whole universe from within.

As Arthur Peacocke writes: 'we are that part of the cosmos consciously capable of being aware of and of responding to that immanent Presence'.[72] Human beings, then, are creatures in whom the process of the whole universe reaches its goal, and, because we live in a graced universe, this goal is nothing less than intimacy with the Creator.

In human beings the cosmos experiences God's free self-communication, and is invited into enduring relationship. This experience of grace gives us hope of a future glory which will be the fulfilment of human and cosmic life. The God who is at work in the becoming of the universe is drawing the cosmos towards a future which is both unpredictable, and a fulfilment beyond all hopes.

But we come up against the terrible contradiction of sin. Human beings are not at ease with their environment, or within themselves. They live in tension with one another, and, at the end of the twentieth century, find themselves in a situation where the life-systems of the Earth are threatened by human activity. Human beings consistently fall short of fulfilling their potential. They compete with one another, exploit one another and abuse other creatures, regardless of the consequences. They make war on one another and on the life-systems of the planet. They come up against the limits of human existence, above all death, and because these limits are too hard to endure with full consciousness, they are repressed, and reveal themselves in alienated and damaging ways.

Human beings find themselves in an alienated state, – from the rest of creatures, from one another, from themselves, and from the divine ground of all being. This situation constitutes a need for wholeness and healing, for liberation and reconciliation. Theologically, we call this alienated condition 'original sin', and we call our conscious choices for alienation 'personal sin'. Humankind is in need of healing and reconciliation at the most profound level.

Humanity looks for liberation. Christianity's claim is that the God who is at the heart of the unfolding cosmos has become part of human history in Jesus of Nazareth, bringing salvation and healing to the whole world. Through the life, death and resurrection of Jesus, the transfiguration of our world has begun. Christianity further claims that this same God touches, surrounds and embraces every person at every moment through the outpouring of the Holy Spirit. God's self-offering in love to each human person can be freely accepted or rejected. To say 'yes' to this offer either explicitly, or implicitly by fidelity to conscience, is to be taken into a justifying and liberating relationship with the living God.

The movement at the heart of cosmic processes does not reach its fulfilment simply in human life or in human history, but only in that embrace between Creator and creatures which Christians call grace. The history of the universe reaches its climax when the creative Ground of the whole cosmic process engages in self-giving love with the universe come to consciousness in free human persons.

We live in a world of grace, a world in which God is present in self-offering at every point. Every act of knowing, every question, every free decision, every experience of love, every moment of wonder, is an opening to the holy mystery which comes close to us in love.

The experience of the overwhelming size and bounty of the universe, the experience of the unity and inter-relationship of all things, the experience of friendship, the experience of compassion and the shared struggle for justice, the experience of solitude, the experience of loss and death, the experience of limits and the experience of the transcendence of the human spirit, these and many other experiences open women and men to the mystery which is at the heart of human existence in the universe.

Christian revelation tells us that in these experiences we are encountering signs of the presence of what Jesus called the 'kingdom of God'. A God of unconditional love, of unbounded compassion, turns towards us in self-offering. Our existence is encompassed by this mystery which stands revealed as limitless love. Sheer grace surrounds us at every point. Grace is the heartbeat of the universe. It is God bent over us with love.

The story of the cosmos and the story of humankind is a single story. The unfolding, evolutionary history of the cosmos involves not only the movement from matter to life, and the movement from life to self-consciousness, but also the experience by conscious and free persons of God's self-communication by grace.

If human beings are the cosmos come to consciousness before the grace of God, if they are the self-transcendence of matter, if they are already contained in some way in the cosmic fireball, if they are truly made from stardust, then they are profoundly interconnected with birds and rain forests, with insects and whales, with photosynthesis and river systems, with hydrogen atoms and the great Milky Way galaxy.

FURTHER REFLECTION

1. How do you respond to the picture, presented here, of human beings in inter-relationship with other creatures? What elements do you find appealing or helpful? Where do you see serious questions arising? Where is there need for development?

2. Karl Rahner has said that the scientific view of the emergence and size of the cosmos can induce a kind of 'cosmic dizziness'. How might we respond to this experience of cosmic dizziness as people of faith? What effect does it have on your understanding of God? What about God's relationship with human beings?

3. Does this overview 'make sense' to you in the context of the discoveries of cosmology, and in the light of your faith? How would you like to see it modified or developed?

4 To what extent do you see this kind of theology as providing a basis for a Christian theological approach to ecology? What would you see as fundamental to such an approach? What would it involve for you?

CHAPTER 4

Concluding remarks

This book began with the global crisis of the late twentieth century, and the urgent need to rethink the way human beings inter-relate with other creatures on Earth. It seems to me that this rethinking is an absolute necessity and that every person, and every discipline, trade and profession, is called upon to take part in it. I have taken it for granted that, for Christian believers, it is essential that theology play its part in this renewal in human self-understanding.

In the first part of this book I have argued that an adequate theology of the human person is needed as an alternative to the kind of anthropocentric thinking which justifies irresponsible exploitation and pollution of the Earth, and which, at a deeper level, alienates human beings from the community of creatures. It is needed, as well, as an alternative to those who view human beings as simply one species among others, or who see us as a plague upon the Earth.

In a brief study of the biblical tradition on creation I have taken the position that Christian believers are not bound to the scientific frameworks of the biblical authors, nor to the sequence of the literary construct of the seven days of the first creation story. What we *are* bound to are the key theological teachings of the biblical accounts of creation. I have made a summary of key insights which emerge from the story of creation in Genesis 1-2:4, and then, more briefly, from the stories of Genesis 2-11, from Psalm 104, and from some of the most important New Testament texts concerned with the relationship between Jesus and creation. All of this provides the illumination by which a Christian believer can ponder the story of creation which emerges from late twentieth-century science, and move towards a new theological picture.

I have argued that we can build a theology of the human person in inter-relationship with the rest of creation by taking into account six dimensions of human beings: that they have their origin with all creatures in the great primordial fireball; that they are made from stardust; that they are part of the evolutionary history of life on Earth; that they are companions with other creatures in an Earth community; that they are the universe come to self-consciousness at a particular place and time; that they are part of the universe invited into relationship with the living God, through God's gracious and free self-offering.

It seems to me that when the human person is understood in this way, then we have a viable alternative to extreme anthropocentrism. In the theological view argued in this book, all of creation exists in complex networks of inter-relationship and the human community is part of this earthly and cosmic community. Each creature has its own part to play, each species has its own value. All are interconnected within an ecological whole. Here human beings are understood within the integrity of God's creation. If this view is taken seriously, then the integrity of creation becomes a new ethical norm governing all human behaviour. This means, in the words of John Paul II, that 'we cannot interfere in one area of the ecosystem without paying due attention both to the consequences of such interference in other areas and to the well-being of future generations'.[73]

The integrity of creation is grounded not simply on our interconnection with all other creatures in an Earth community, and a cosmic community, but in the one God who is present to all creatures, sustaining and empowering them. It is grounded in the incarnation by which the Word of God is forever bodily, forever matter, and in the conviction that the whole material universe is being transfigured in and through the risen Christ. It is grounded in the fact that every creature is sacramental, revealing and embodying something of the mystery and the diversity of the Creator. If this is taken seriously then, as Thomas Berry has said, 'to wantonly destroy a living species is to silence forever a divine voice'.[74]

On the other hand, the kind of vision of the human person within creation developed here stresses not only the human community's inter-relationship with all other creatures but also the dignity and value of human persons as those in whom the universe comes to self-awareness before the gracious offer of God's friendship. This is far removed from levelling or reductionist views of the human person. The ancient biblical principle of the dignity of the human person made in the image of God not only retains its relevance, but is given new force in the cosmic perspective I have outlined in this book. Being made in the image of God means being called to be in solidarity and companionship with the living God in this God's presence to, and care for, all creatures. It means being invited to become 'friends of the Friend of the world'.[75] The dignity of the human person remains the fundamental principle undergirding the quest for social justice on our planet.

Social justice and the well-being of the planet are not competing options, but part of the one ethical stance. We all know how the appalling injustice of the international debt structure is directly related not only to the misery of so many people in our world, but also to the destruction of great rain forests and to other ecological disasters in third-world countries. We know, too, that recent wars have led not only to horrifying deaths and injuries, but also to massive damage to the land, to the sea and to the atmosphere.

There can be only one option for humanity in our times, an option faithful to the theological view of the human person developed here, the option which finds expression in the commitment of the World Council of Churches to 'Justice, Peace and the Integrity of Creation'.

We live in a time of unparalleled crisis, but there is hope for our world, a hope based upon God's action at the heart of all things, a hope based, too, upon the ways in which God's kingdom is already present in anticipatory and partial ways in our world: in all those working for a just and peaceful world, in those who commit themselves to the work of opposing racism and sexism, in those whose love and work builds inclusive community, in the world-wide consciousness among ordinary people that the life-systems of the Earth really matter, in the work of activists, in the lives of gardeners and farmers who love and respect the land, and in the cultures of indigenous peoples like the Australian Aborigines. In these and many other ways, God is already at work in our human community in all that might be gathered up in our one option for justice, peace and the integrity of creation.

> Listen carefully, careful
> and this spirit e come in your feeling
> and you will feel it...anyone that.
> I feel it...my body same as you.
> I telling you this because the land for us,
> never change round, never change.
> Places for us, earth for us,
> star, moon, tree, animal,
> no-matter what sort of an animal, bird or snake...
> all that animal same like us. Our friend that.[76]

FURTHER REFLECTION

1. What do you think about the claim that commitment to ecology and commitment to the poor of the Earth need to be held together? How do you see their inter-relationship in your own life?

2. How do you see the relationship between the ecological movement and the feminist movement? What are the points of interconnection? How do you relate them at the level of theology?

3. What is your picture of an ecologically sustainable life-style?

4. What does all of this mean in terms of your own commitment to justice, peace and the integrity of creation? What action has priority for you?

NOTES

---

*

1   For a clear picture of the crisis we face, and the interconnections between ecological issues and international justice see Sean McDonagh, *To Care for the Earth*, Bear and Co., Santa Fe 1986 and *The Greening of the Church*, Canterbury Press, Scoresby, Vic. 1990.

2   Bill Neidjie, *Story About Feeling*, Magabala Books, Broome, W.A., 1989, pp.2–4.

3   Edward Schillebeeckx has some useful comments on this in his *Church: The Human Story of God* Crossroad, New York, 1990, pp. 240–246.

4   See, for example, Thomas Aquinas, *Summa Theologiae*, 1.47.1. Some of the greatest expressions of this attitude to creation can be found in the prayers of ancient Israel, above all in Psalm 104.

5   At this point, I take a different view to Thomas Berry, although I find his work full of desperately-needed insight. See his *The Dream Of the Earth*, Sierra Club Books, San Francisco, 1988, p.209.

6   I will need to cover some of the same material discussed in a recent book, *Jesus and the Cosmos: Exploring Themes from Rahner for an Ecological Age*, Paulist Press, New York, and St. Paul, Homebush, NSW, 1991. The concerns of *Jesus and the Cosmos* are Christological and, in this present work, my focus will be on theological anthropology rather than on the theology of Jesus Christ. They are, of course, closely inter-related.

7   I have followed Claus Westermann here. See his *Creation*, Fortress Press, Philadelphia, 1974, p.42.

8   For many years, Church authorities have encouraged a process of biblical interpretation which respects literary forms and cultural assumptions. For the official Roman Catholic view on this, see the encyclical of Pius XII, *Divino Afflante Spiritu*, 1943, *The Instruction Concerning the Historical Truth of the Gospels*

from the Pontifical Biblical Commission, 1964 and Vatican II's *Dogmatic Constitution on Divine Revelation*, par.12.

9 Bruce Vawter, *On Genesis: A New Reading*, Doubleday, New York, 1977, p.48.

10 Walter Brueggemann, *Genesis: Interpretation: A Bible Commentary for Teaching and Preaching*, John Knox Press, Atlanta, 1982, p.17.

11 ibid., p.27.

12 Claus Westermann, *Blessing in the Bible and the Life of the Church*, Fortress Press, Philadelphia, 1978.

13 Gordon Wenham, for example, considers five solutions to the problem of the meaning of 'image of God' and suggests that the strongest case is made for the meaning that the human person is God's vice-regent on Earth. See his *Word Biblical Commentary: Genesis 1–15*, Word Books, Waco, Texas, 1987, pp.29–32.

14 Claus Westermann, *Creation*, p.56.

15 Karl Barth, *Kirchliche Dogmatik* III,1, p.206. See Claus Westermann, *Creation*, p.58.

16 To 'have dominion' translates the Hebrew verb *radah*, which is a strong expression, usually associated with kingly rule (I Kings 5:3, Ps. 72:8; 110:2; Is.14:6; Ezek. 34:4). Bruce Vawter (*On Genesis*, p.60) says of the word 'subdue': "Subdue" (*kabas*) is part of the same uncompromising rhetoric within which "have dominion" falls: literally it implies trampling under one's feet, and it connotes absolute subjugation (cf. Jeremiah, 34:11–16; Zecheriah 9:15; Nehemiah 5:5; 2 Chronicles 28:10).

17 John Paul II, *On Human Work*, St. Paul, Homebush, NSW, 1981, pp.19–43; *On Social Concerns*, St. Paul, Homebush, NSW, 1988, pp.61–64; *Peace with God the Creator; Peace with All of Creation*, St. Paul, Homebush, NSW, 1990, pp.3–5.

18 See John Paul II, *On the Dignity and Vocation of Women*, St. Paul, Homebush NSW, 1988, pp.28–31.

19 Walter Brueggemann, *Genesis*, p.35.

20 See Claus Westermann, *Creation*, pp.64–65.

21 Biblical scholars believe that the second story of origins comes from the Yahwist source (J) which goes back to the tenth century BC. The J material is found in Gen. 2–3, 4, 11:1–9, as well as in

parts of the flood story and the genealogies. As has been said, it seems that the first creation story (1:1–2:4a) comes from the priestly source (P) in the seventh to sixth centuries BC. It appears that P is also the source of parts of the flood narrative and the genealogies. The theme from P of the image of God appears not only in 1:26–27, but also after the expulsion from the garden (5:1) and after the flood (9:6).

22 See Lawrence Boadt, 'The Pentateuch' in the *The Catholic Study Bible*, Oxford University Press, New York, 1990, pp.59–61.

23 For a very helpful exposition of Paul's theology of new creation and its contemporary relevance see Brendan Byrne, *Inheriting the Earth: The Pauline Basis for a Spirituality for Our Time*, St. Paul, Homebush, NSW, 1990.

24 In many cosmological theories, the beginning of the universe is thought of as a 'singularity'. In a singularity the density of the universe and the curvature of space–time would be infinite and mathematics would lose its meaning. Stephen Hawking who, with Roger Penrose, had earlier argued for a 'big bang' singularity now believes that there is no need for a singularity at the beginning of space–time. Rather 'space and time together might form a finite, four-dimensional space without singularities or boundaries, like the surface of the earth but with more dimensions'. See his *A Brief History of Time: From the Big Bang to Black Holes*, Bantam Press, London, 1988, p.173.

25 Stephen Hawking, *A Brief History of Time*, p.118.

26 Recent astronomical evidence suggests that galaxies are formed in huge bubble-like structures, with sheets of galaxies wrapped around relatively empty areas, and with the great bubbles surrounded by filaments of further galaxies. Researchers have also come to the conclusion that the Local Supercluster of galaxies, which includes our own, is moving in a motion which is distinct from the expected 'Hubble flow' of the expanding universe, apparently pulled by an immense concentration of matter known as the Great Attractor at a speed of 650 kilometres per second. For most scientists these discoveries call for a rethinking of the 'big bang', but they do not call into question the model of the 'big bang' itself. Swedish physicist, Hannes Alfven is one of a small minority of scientists who oppose the 'big bang' model. He argues that galaxies are the result of

magnetic fields induced by electrical currents flowing through plasma, and he suggests that the universe may have existed infinitely.

27 Theorists speak of a number of 'eras' in the first second. They name the period of the universe between 10^{-43} and 10^{-35} second as the **GUT Era**. GUT refers to the 'grand unification theories' of physicists, who think that, in this period, the electromagnetic and the strong and weak nuclear forces were still unified. Gravity may have emerged with its separate identity at the beginning of the GUT Era. The GUT Era was followed by the **Inflation Era** (10^{-35} to 10^{-33} second) which will be described in the text, and at the end of this period the separation of the four forces was completed in what is called the **Electroweak Era**. In the next period, the **Quark Confinement Era** between 10^{-6} and 2 seconds, gluons of the strong nuclear force enabled quarks to coalesce into nuclear particles – protons, neutrons and their antiparticles. It was during this period that the excess of matter over antimatter, which dates from the Inflation Era became critical, as few new particle pairs were produced, and matter and antimatter particles annihilated one another.

28 Paul Davies points out that 'during this incredibly brief phase the region of space which today forms the entire observable universe grew from one-thousand-millionth of the size of a proton to several centimetres'. See his *Superforce: The Search for a Grand Unified Theory of Nature*, Unwin Paperbacks, London, 1985, p.192. The inflationary theory was introduced by Alan Guth, and later developed by Andrei Linde. Cosmologists have developed theories about the beginnings of the universe on the basis of the quantum physics of vacuums. In quantum physics, the vacuum is regarded as a ferment of quantum activity. A number of scientists speculate that the universe had its origin in an extremely rapid inflation from an excited vacuum state. If it is assumed that in the beginning the universe was in an excited vacuum state (what is sometimes called a 'false' vacuum) then this excited vacuum state could result in a powerful cosmic repulsion force that would cause very rapid expansion. On the basis of this theory, Paul Davies describes the first fraction of a second: 'In the beginning the universe erupted spontaneously out of nothing. From a featureless ferment of

quantum energy, bubbles of empty space began to inflate at accelerating pace, bootstrapping colossal reserves of energy into existence. This false vacuum, infused with self-created energy, was unstable and began to decay, dumping its energy in the form of heat, filling each bubble with a fireball. Inflation ceased, but the big bang was started. The time was 10^{-32}s.' (*Superforce*, p.204). In a recent book, Roger Penrose places the inflationary theory firmly in the 'tentative' category. See his *The Emperor's New Mind: Concerning Computers, Minds, and the Laws of Physics*, Vintage, London, 1989, p.200. See also note 13 on p.449.

29 See Paul Davies, *Superforce*, p.181.

30 Penzias and Wilson were testing a new, extremely sensitive microwave detector. This discovery confirmed predictions made in 1948 by George Gamow and Ralph Alpher.

31 Absolute zero is the lowest possible temperature. At absolute zero a substance contains no heat energy. Absolute temperature is a measure of the thermal energy of particles.

32 Thomas Berry, *The Dream of the Earth*, pp.196-197.

33 Burbridge, Burbridge, Fowler and Hoyle in *Reviews of Modern Physics* 29 (1957), p.547.

34 Bernard Lovell, *In the Centre of Immensities*, Hutchinson, London, 1979, p.23.

35 Nucleosynthesis in stars cannot account for the abundance of helium in the universe. Steven Weinberg writes in *the First Three Minutes* (Bantam Books, New York, 1977): 'today it is generally believed that nucleosynthesis occurs *both* cosmologically and in stars; the helium and perhaps a few other light nuclei were synthesized in the early universe, while the stars were responsible for everything else.'

36 Paul Davies, *Superforce*, p.171.

37 David Ellyard, *Sky Watch*, ABC, Crows Next, NSW, 1988, p.85.

38 See John Gribbin's comments in *In Search of the Big Bang: Quantum Physics and Cosmology*, Corgi Books, London, 1986, p. 177.

39 See Arthur Peacocke, *God and the New Biology*, J.M. Dent, London, 1986, p.145.

40 ibid., p.35.

41 ibid., p.36.

42 James Lovelock, *Gaia: A New Look at Life On Earth*, Oxford University Press, 1979; *The Ages of Gaia: A Biography of Our Living Earth*, W.W. Norton, New York, 1988.

43 See G. Nicolis and I. Prigogine, *Self-Organization in Non-Equilibrium Systems* Wiley, New York, 1977; Ilya Prigogine and Isobelle Stengers, *Order Out of Chaos* Heinemann, London, 1984; M. Eigen and P. Schuster, *The Hypercycle* Springer-Verlag, Heidelberg, 1979.

44 On all of this, see Paul Davies, *The Cosmic Blueprint,* Unwin, London, 1987, and Arthur Peacocke, *God and the New Biology,* pp.133–160.

45 In my own Catholic tradition, the theory of evolution is an open question, as long as related doctrines (like the spiritual nature of the human person and original sin) are safe-guarded. This was made explicit by Pope Pius XII in his encyclical, *Humani Generis* in 1950. While stating that evolution was an 'open question', the Pope repeated the Catholic teaching that human souls are immediately created by God. Since then, theologians like Karl Rahner have sought to show that the special nature of God's action in creating spiritual human beings can be understood as God dynamically present as the power of active self-transcendence at the heart of evolution, bringing the whole process to the point of the emergence of uniquely spiritual human beings. This seems to preserve the essentials of the tradition of the special creation of the human soul, without requiring extraordinary or miraculous intervention by God in the arena of secondary causes. For a thorough treatment of all of this in terms of Catholic doctrine, see Michael Schmaus *Dogma 2: God and Creation*, Sheed and Ward, London, 1969, pp.122–144. With regard to the issue of polygenism, Pius XII wrote in *Humani Generis*, 'It does not appear how such views can be reconciled with the doctrine of original sin, as this is guaranteed to us by scripture and tradition, and proposed to us by the Church.' This is an important judgement for Catholic theology, but it does not amount to an absolute or final rejection of polygenism. According to Karl Rahner (and many other theologians) 'one may well hold that in the meantime the

development of Catholic theology has advanced so far that the compatibility of polygenism may be prudently maintained.' This position, which represents a development in Rahner's own thinking, can be found argued in the article on 'monogenism' in K. Rahner (ed.) *Encyclopedia of Theology: A Concise Sacramentum Mundi*, Burns and Oates, London, 1975, pp.974–977.

46 Charles Birch, *On Purpose*, New South Wales University Press, Kensington, NSW, 1990, pp.23–24. See also Charles Birch, William Eakin and Jay B. McDaniel (eds.) *Liberating Life: Contemporary Approaches to Ecological Theology*, Orbis Press, Maryknoll, New York, 1990.

47 See Paul Davies, *The Cosmic Blueprint*, Unwin, London, 1987, repr. 1989. For a detailed study of the mind from the point of view of modern physics, see Roger Penrose, *The Emperor's New Mind*.

48 N. Bohr, *Atomic Physics, and the Description of Nature*, Cambridge University Press, London, 1934, p.57.

49 David Bohm, *Wholeness and the Implicate Order*, Routledge and Kegan Paul, London, 1980, p.9. See Charles Birch, *On Purpose*, p.79.

50 Fritjof Capra, *The Tao of Physics*, Fontana, London, 1975, repr. 1983, p.150.

51 Sallie McFague, *Models of God: Theology for an Ecological, Nuclear Age*, Fortress Press, Philadelphia, 1987, p.11.

52 ibid., p.9.

53 Thomas Berry, *The Dream of the Earth*, p.196.

54 These themes are developed in an article by Michael Himes and Kenneth Himes, 'The Sacrament of Creation: Towards an Environmental Theology', in *Commonweal* 117, 26 Jan, 1990, pp.42–49. See also Tony Kelly, 'Wholeness, Ecological and Catholic?' in *Pacifica* 3, June, 1990, pp.201–223.

55 Matthew Fox's recent work includes *Original Blessing: A Primer in Creation Spirituality* Bear and Co., Santa Fe, 1983 ; *The Coming of the Cosmic Christ* Collins Dove, Melbourne 1988, *Creation Spirituality: Liberating Gifts for the Peoples of the Earth* Harper Collins, New York, 1991.

56 From Marion A. Habig (ed.), *St. Francis of Assisi: Writings and*

Early Biographies, Franciscan Press, Chicago, 1983, pp.130–131.

57 Sean McDonagh, *The Greening of the Church*, p.173.

58 John of the Cross, *The Spiritual Canticle,* in *The Collected Works of St. John of the Cross*, tr. by Kieran Kavanaugh and Otilio Rodriguez, ICS Publications, Washington, D.C., 1979, p.473.

59 Teilhard de Chardin, *The Phenomenon of Man*, William Collins, London, 1959, p.243.

60 Thomas Berry, *The Dream of the Earth*, p.198.

61 Sallie McFague, *Models of God*, p.76.

62 Carl Sagan, *Cosmos*, Ballantine Books, New York, 1980, p.286.

63 Paul Davies, *Superforce*, p.204.

64 Arthur Peacocke, *God and the New Biology*, p.126.

65 ibid., p.91.

66 Karl Rahner, *Foundations of Christian Faith*, Seabury Press, New York, 1978, pp.188–189.

67 This is what Teilhard de Chardin called the 'noosphere'. See, for example, his *Future of Man*, Harper and Row, New York, 1947, p.164. Emily Binns has recently developed a theology of creation within this tradition in *The World as Creation: Creation in Christ in an Evolutionary World View*, Michael Glazier, Wilmington, Delaware, 1990.

68 As Paul Davies has said: 'the knowledge that our presence in the universe represents a *fundamental* rather than an *incidental* feature of existence offers, I believe, a deep and satisfying basis for human dignity.' *The Cosmic Blueprint*, p.203.

69 Thomas Berry, *The Dream of the Earth*, p.132. See also pp.16 and 128.

70 Paul Davies, *The Cosmic Blueprint*, p.203.

71 In parts of this section, I am following quite closely a line of thought I have already expressed in chapter 3 of *Jesus and the Cosmos*.

72 Arthur Peacocke, *God and the New Biology*, p.129.

73 Pope John Paul II, *Peace with God the Creator; Peace with all of Creation*, p.5.

74 The Dream of the Earth, p.46.
75 This is an expression of Sallie McFague's. See *Models of God*, p.172.
76 Bill Neidjie, *Story About Feeling*, p.19.

FURTHER READING

*

Barrow, John, and Silk, Joseph. *The Left Hand of Creation.* Basic Books, New York, 1983.

Berry Thomas. *The Dream of the Earth.* Sierra Club Books, San Francisco, 1988.

Berry, Thomas, with Clark, Thomas. *Befriending the Earth: A Theology of Reconciliation between Humans and the Earth.* Twenty-third Publications, Connecticut, 1991.

Birch, Charles. *On Purpose.* New South Wales University Press, Kensington, NSW, 1990.

— — Eakin, William and McDaniel, Jay B. (editors). *Liberating Life: Contemporary Approaches to Ecological Theology.*Orbis Books, Maryknoll, New York, 1990.

Brueggemann, Walter. *Genesis: Interpretation: A Bible Commentary for Teaching and Preaching.* John Knox Press, Atlanta, 1982.

Daly, Gabriel. *Creation and Redemption.* Gill and Macmillan, Dublin, 1988.

Davies, Paul. *The Cosmic Blueprint.* Unwin Paperbacks, London, 1987, 1989.

— — *God and the New Physics.* Viking Penguin, New York, 1983.

— — *Superforce: The Search for a Grand Unified Theory of Nature.* Simon and Schuster, New York, 1984.

de Chardin, Teilhard. *The Phenomenon of Man.* Harper, New York, 1959.

Edwards, Denis. *Jesus and the Cosmos: Exploring Themes from Rahner for an Ecological Age.* Paulist Press, Mahwah, New Jersey, 1981.

Fox, Matthew. *Creation Spirituality: Liberating Gifts for the Peoples of the Earth.* Harper Collins, New York, 1991.

— — *Original Blessing: A Primer in Creation Spirituality.* Bear and Co., Santa Fe, 1993.

Gribben, John. *In Search of the Big Bang*. Bantam, New York, 1986.

—— and Rees, Martin. *Cosmic Coincidences: Dark Matter, Mankind and Anthropic Cosmology*. Black Swan, London, 1991. Originally published as *The Stuff of the Universe*. William Heinemann, London, 1990.

Lovell, Bernard. *In the Centre of Immensities*. Hutchinson, London, 1978.

Hawking, Stephen. *A Brief History of Time: From the Big Bang to Black Holes*.Bantam Press, New York, 1988.

McDonagh, Sean. *The Greening of the Church*. Canterbury Press, Scoresby, Vic. 1990.

—— *To Care for the Earth: A Call to a New Theology*. Bear and Company, Santa Fe, New Mexico, 1986.

McFague, Sallie. *Models of God: Theology for an Ecological, Nuclear Age*. Fortress Press, Philadelphia, 1987.

Moltmann, Jurgen. *God in Creation: An Ecological Doctrine of Creation*. SCM Press, London, 1984.

Parker, Barry. Creation: *The Story of the Origin and Evolution of the Universe*. Plenum Press, New York, 1988.

Peacocke, Arthur. *God and the New Biology*. J.M. Dent and Sons Ltd, London, 1986.

Peter, Ted (editor). *Cosmos as Creation: Theology and Science in Consonance*. Abingdon Press, Nashville, 1989.

Polkinghorne, John. *Reason and Reality: The Relationship Between Science and Theology*. SPCK, London, 1991.

—— *Science and Creation: The Search for Understanding*. London, SPCK, 1988.

Prigogine, Ilya and Stengers, Isabelle. *Order our of Chaos: Man's New Dialogue with Nature*. Fontana Paperbacks, London. 1984.

Rahner, Karl. 'Christology Within an Evolutionary View of the World. *Theological Investigations V* Helicon Press, Baltimore, 1966, pp. 157-192.

—— Natural Science and Reasonable Faith: Theological Perspectives for Dialogue with the Natural Sciences. *Theological Investigations XXI* Crossroad, New York. 1988, pp. 16-55.

Ruether, Rosemary. *Sexism and God-Talk: Towards a Feminist Theology*. SCM, London, 1983.

Russell, Robert John, Stoeger, William R. and Coyne, George V. (editors). *Physics, Philosophy and Theology: A Common Quest for Understanding.* Vatican Observatory, Vatican City State, 1988.

Silk, Joseph. *The Big Band.* Freeman, San Francisco, 1980.

Waggoner, Robert and Goldsmith, Donald. *Cosmic Horizons: Understanding the Universe.* Stanford University Press, Stanford, 1982.

Weinberg, Steven. *The First Three Minutes.* Bantam Books, New York, 1977.

Westermann, Claus. *Creation.* Fortress Press, Philadelphia, 1974.